JOHN MAYER HEAVIER THINGS

Piano/Vocal arrangements by John Nicholas

Album art direction by John Mayer
Graphics by Ames Design
Album artwork courtesy of Sony Records
Cover photo by Chapman Baehler

Cherry Lane Music Company
Director of Publications/Project Editor: Mark Phillips
Manager of Publications: Rebecca Quigley

ISBN 1-57560-714-X

Visit our website at www.cherrylane.com

JOHN MAYER GETS INTO SOME *HEAVIER THINGS*

When John Mayer emerged from the underground in 2001 with his debut album, *Room for Squares,* he was a little-known 22-year-old with an acoustic guitar and boundless energy. His ascent was rapid, powered by nonstop touring and intensive word of mouth, which reached critical mass just as radio and the video channels were discovering the young artist. Two years later, *Room for Squares* was triple-platinum (the album remained in the Top 100 after more than 80 consecutive weeks on the *Billboard* Top 200 chart), spawning three hit singles, one of which, "Your Body Is a Wonderland," earned him a Grammy in 2003 for Best Pop Vocal Performance.

Mayer's much-anticipated Aware/Columbia follow-up album, which bears the intriguing title *Heavier Things,* demonstrates how far this single-minded artist has come at this still-early stage of his career.

"In some ways," Mayer says, "the stakes get higher when you make a second major-label record and everyone's looking. And in some ways absolutely nothing is different, because your voice still sounds the same, and your hands still feel the same on the guitar. You just write your songs. You're just a guy with a guitar putting in a Thai food order at 9 p.m."

The 25-year-old Mayer possesses a remarkable clear-headedness—fittingly, the new album opens with a song titled "Clarity"—and the rarefied level of consciousness that distinguishes this artist's songs has as much to do with their impact as his gift for melody, elevated musicianship, or disarming personality. All of these elements, by the way, are present in spades on *Heavier Things.*

The album was produced and mixed by Jack Joseph Puig, whose credits include Sheryl Crow, No Doubt, the Black Crowes, Hole, and smart-pop progenitors Jellyfish.

"Jack understood what I wanted to do next," Mayer says of his decision to work with Puig. "We had met by way of friendship, not connections. I don't like pulling connections in; I'd much rather make friends. He understands the romance of making records. Jack and I pushed each other to the limits of our knowledge, and that's why the record is as fresh as it is. There are raw decisions made outside of the comfort zone of past achievement."

Heavier Things was tracked in New York, Mayer's present home, and completed at Puig's longtime L.A. headquarters, Ocean Way. In addition to the lead single, the propulsive, hook-packed rocker "Bigger Than My Body," the album contains several songs Mayer performed live on his 2003 summer tour of amphitheaters and arenas—songs that became immediate crowd favorites. These include the poignant "Daughters," the smoldering, blues-based "Come Back to Bed," the evocative "Wheel," and "Something's Missing," which climaxes with a timely and ingenious things-to-do-today inventory.

Mayer's longtime bass player, David LaBruyere, appears on all tracks apart from the virtually solo acoustic "Daughters," while keyboardist Jamie Muhoberac plays on eight. Guest musicians include legendary jazz trumpeter Roy Hargrove, drummers Matt Chamberlain, Steve Jordan, and ?uestlove from the Roots, percussionist Lenny Castro, and horn player Jerry Hay. Also present are guitarist Michael Chaves and drummer J.J. Johnson from Mayer's touring band.

"I came off the road after two years of straight touring and knew exactly what kind of record I wanted to make—it wasn't an accident," Mayer says of the process that led to the creation of *Heavier Things.* "I wanted to write songs this time that always felt good under my hands, no matter what. The only real criterion for the record was, 'Is it fun to play? Is it physically fun to feel the vibration of the strings or the feel of my throat when I'm singing it?' If an idea didn't meet that criterion, it got dumped.

"This record is as different from the last one as I am from the last time I made a record," he adds. "What that amount is, I don't know, and I'm really interested to find out."

KEYWORDS BY SONG

CONTENTS

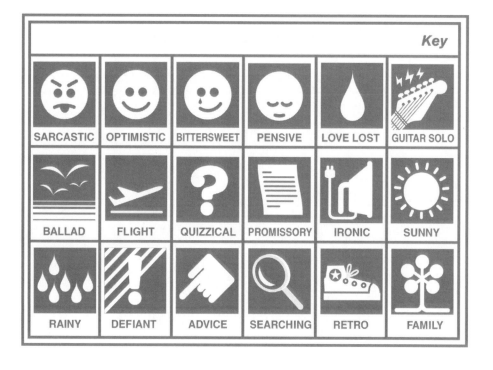

Clarity

Words and Music by
John Mayer

Moderately slow

I wor-

ry   I weigh   three times _ my   bod - y.   I wor -

ry   I throw_ my fear_ a - round.   But this

morn - ing   there's a calm_____ I can't_ ex - plain._

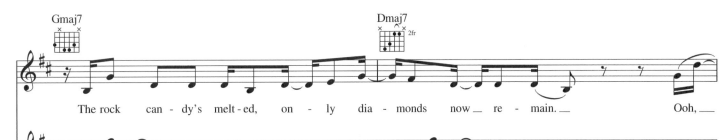

The rock   can - dy's melt - ed,   on - ly dia - monds now_ re - main._   Ooh, ___

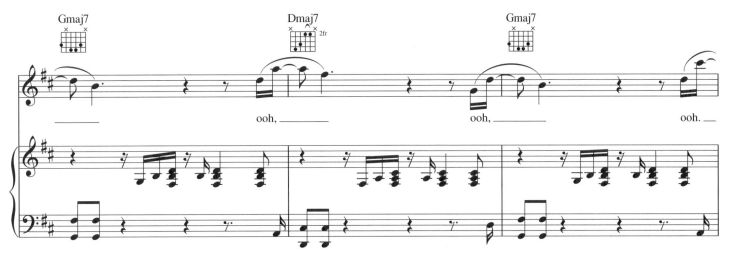

_____   ooh, _____   ooh, _____   ooh. __

By the time I rec-og-nize _ this _

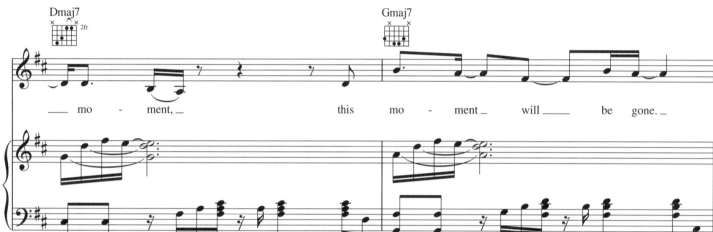

_ mo - ment, _ this mo - ment _ will _ be gone. _

But I will bend the _ light _ pre-tend - ing _

that it some - how _ lin - gered on.

When all __ I got's... __ Ooh, _____ ooh, __

_____ ooh, _____ ooh. _____

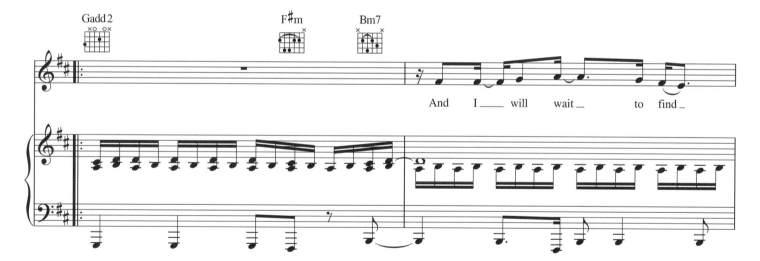

And I __ will wait __ to find __

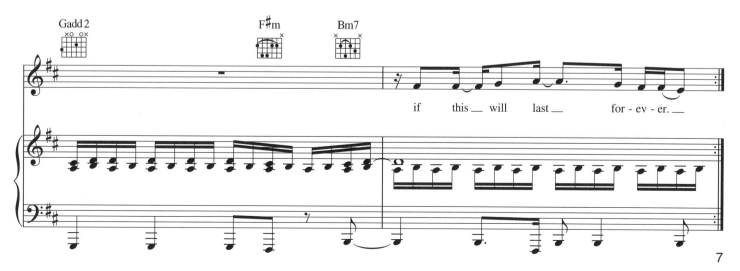

if this __ will last __ for - ev - er. __

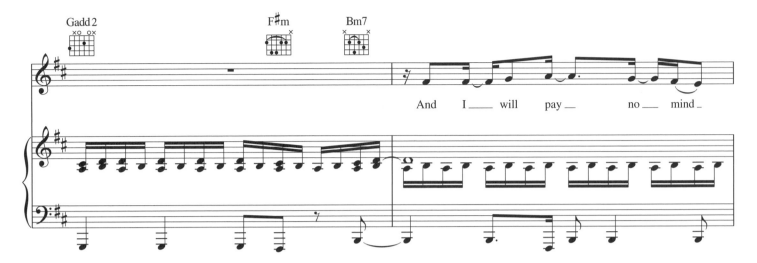

And I ___ will pay ___ no ___ mind ___

when it won't, and it won't be - cause it

can't, ___ it just ___ can't. It's not ___ sup - posed ___

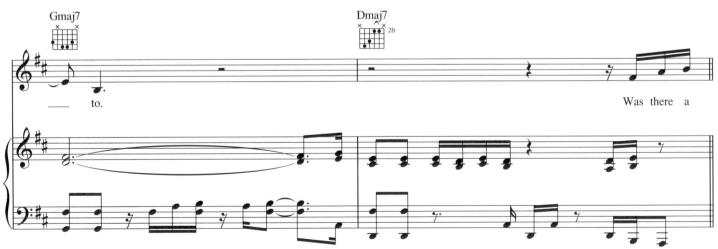

___ to. Was there a

sec - ond of time   I looked ___ a - round? ___   Did I

sail through or drop my an - chor down? ___   Was

an - y - thing ___ e - nough to kiss the ground   and say I'm here

now? ___   And ___ she is here   now. ___   Ooh, ___

ooh, _____ ooh, _____ ooh, __

ooh, _____ ooh. _____ ooh, __

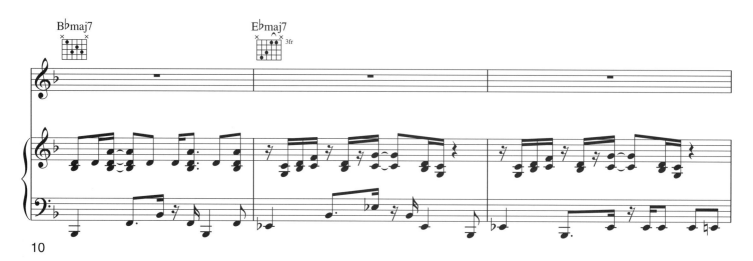

ooh. _____

So much wast - ed in _____ the af -

ter - noon. _____ So much sa -

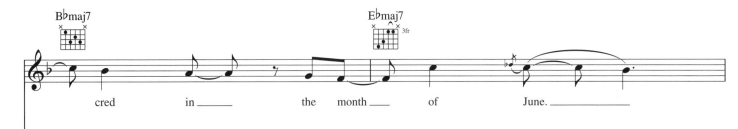

cred in _____ the month _____ of June. _____

How _____ 'bout you? _____ Uh. _____

Ooh,   ha,   ha,   ha,

ha,   ha,   ha,   ha,

ha,   ha,   ooh,   ooh.

Repeat and fade

Vocal ad lib till end

14

Bigger Than My Body

Words and Music by
John Mayer

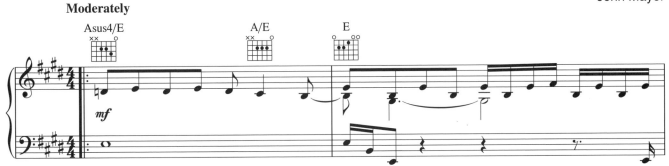

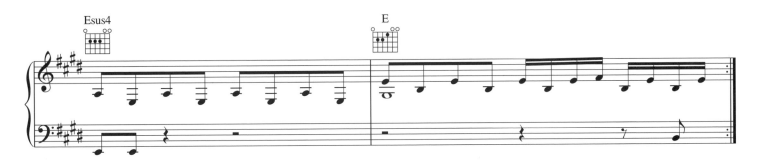

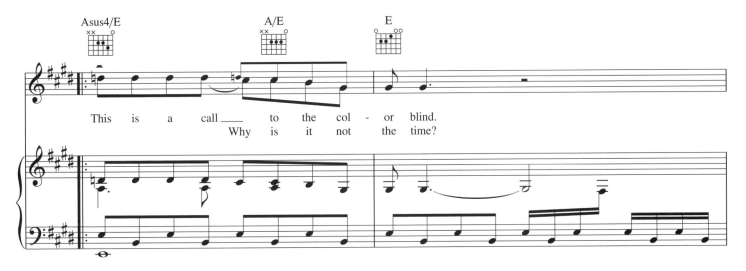

This is a call ___ to the col - or blind.
Why is it not the time?

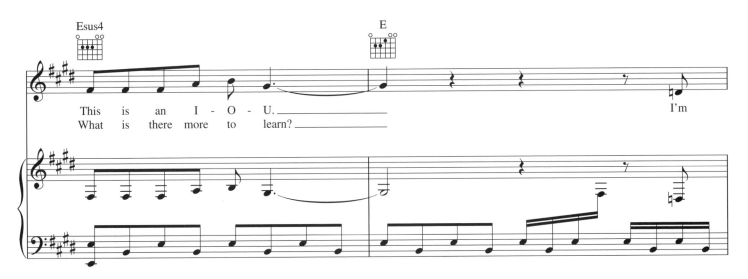

This is an I - O - U. ___
What is there more to learn? ___

I'm

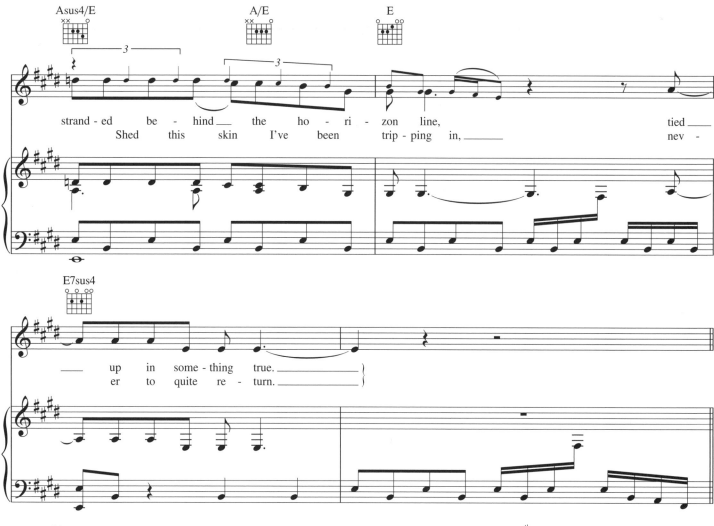

strand-ed be-hind ___ the ho-ri-zon line,   tied ___
Shed this skin I've been trip-ping in, ___   nev-

___ up in some-thing true. ___
er to quite re - turn. ___

Yes, ___ I'm ground-ed,   got ___ my wings ___ clipped.   I'm ___ sur-round-ed by

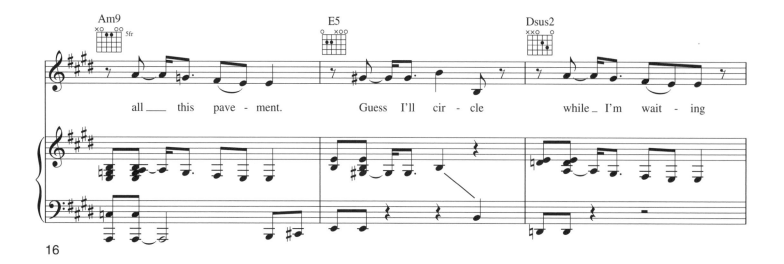

all ___ this pave-ment.   Guess I'll cir-cle   while ___ I'm wait-ing

16

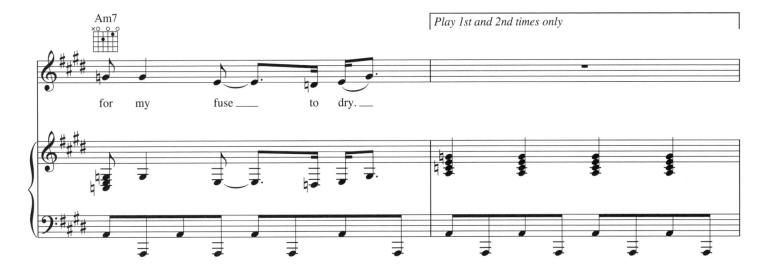

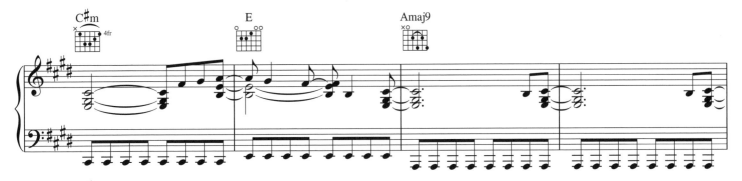

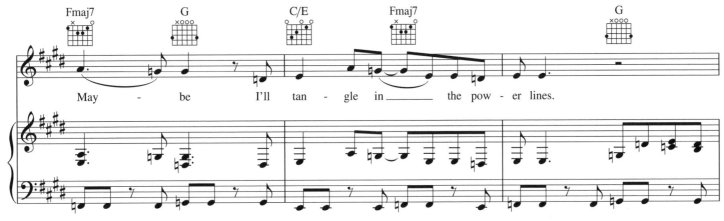

May - be I'll tan - gle in _____ the pow - er lines.

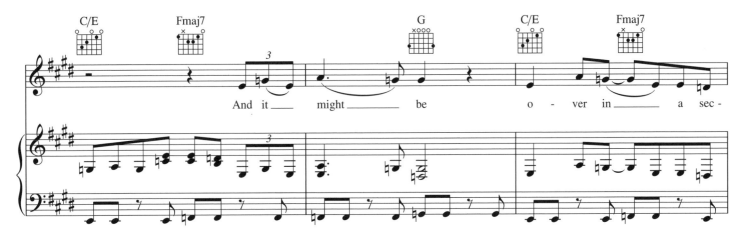

And it _____ might _____ be o - ver in _____ a sec -

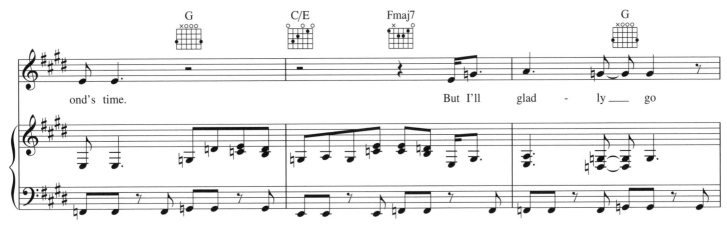

ond's time. But I'll glad - ly _____ go

down in a flame ___ if a flame's ___ what it takes ___ to re-mem-

D.S. al Coda

ber my name, to re-mem-ber my name, ___ yeah.

big-ger ___ than ___ my bod - y. ___ I'm

big-ger ___ than ___ my bod - y. ___ I'm big-ger ___ than ___ my bod-

20

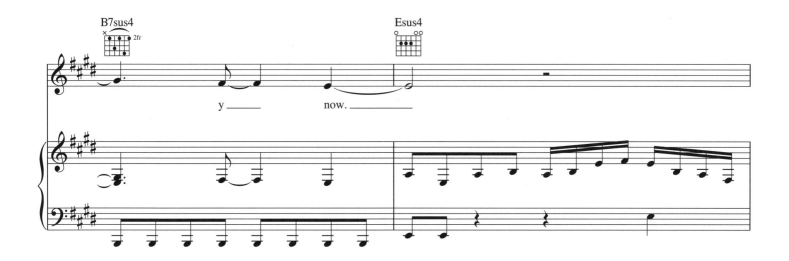

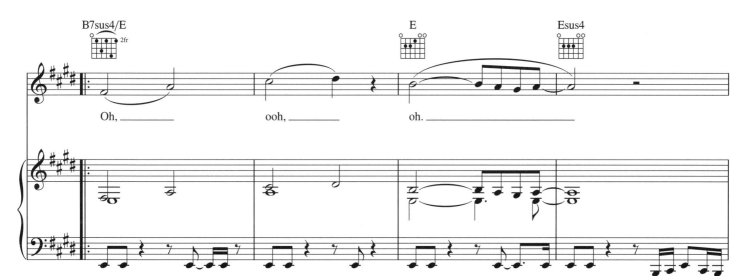

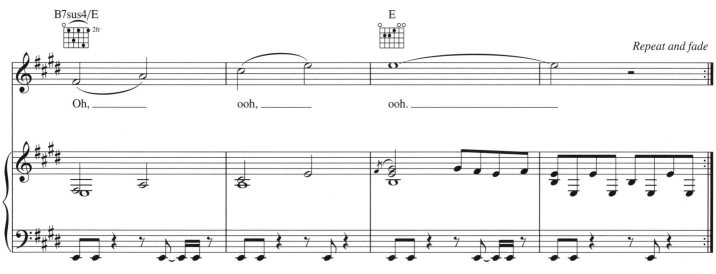

Something's Missing

Words and Music by
John Mayer

Moderately slow

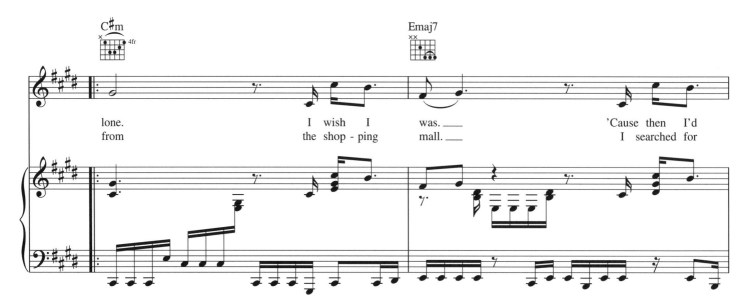

know _____ I was down be - cause I could - n't
joy _____ but I bought it all. It does - n't

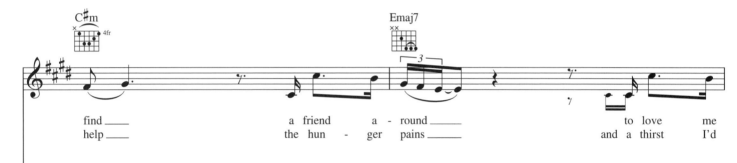

find _____ a friend a - round _____ to love me
help _____ the hun - ger pains _____ and a thirst I'd

1.

like they do right now, they do

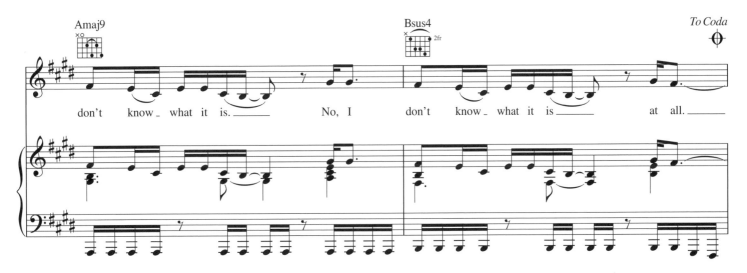

fog in - side the glass _ a - round _____ your sum - mer heart. ___

I can't be sure that this state _____ of mind is not of my own _____

___ de - sign. _____

I

wish there was an o - ver - the - count - er test for lone - li -

ness, for lone - li - ness like _____ this. _____

28

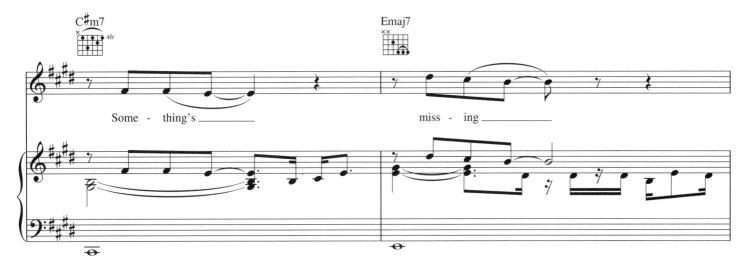

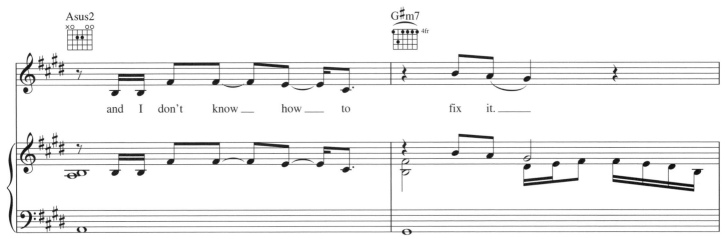

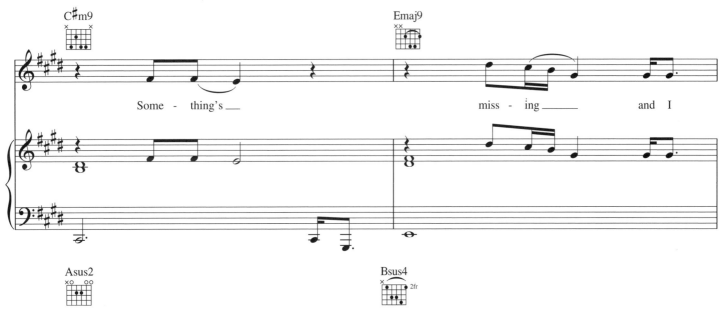

New Deep

Words and Music by
John Mayer

Moderately slow

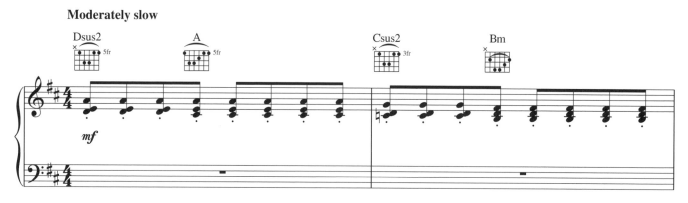

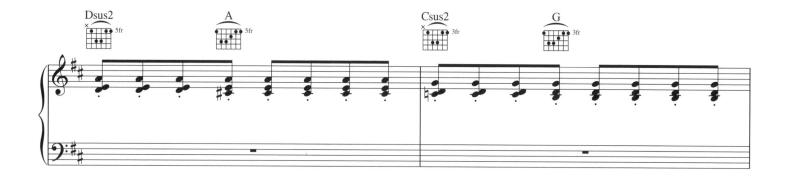

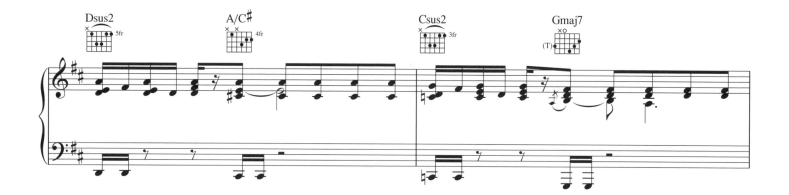

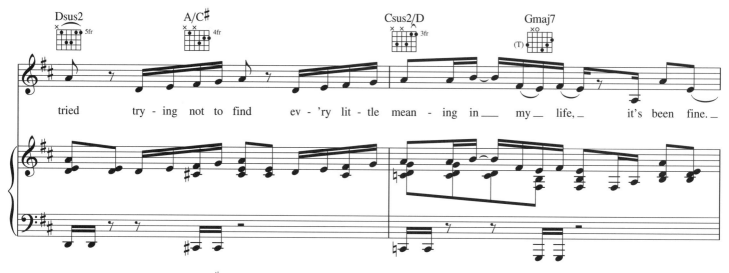

tried   try - ing not to find   ev - 'ry lit - tle mean - ing in ___ my ___ life, ___   it's been fine. ___

___ I've been cool ___ with my   new gold - en ___ rule. ___   Numb is the

new deep.   Done with the old me.   And talk is the

same cheap   it's been. ___

34

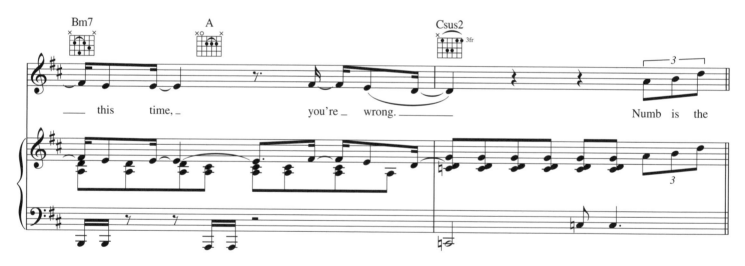

Repeat and fade

Come Back to Bed

Words and Music by
John Mayer

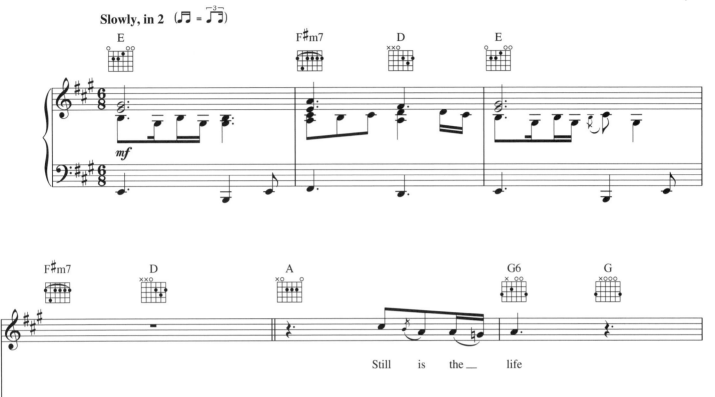

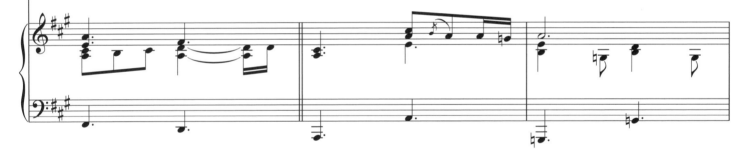

Still is the __ life

of your room   when you're not in -side.   And all of your

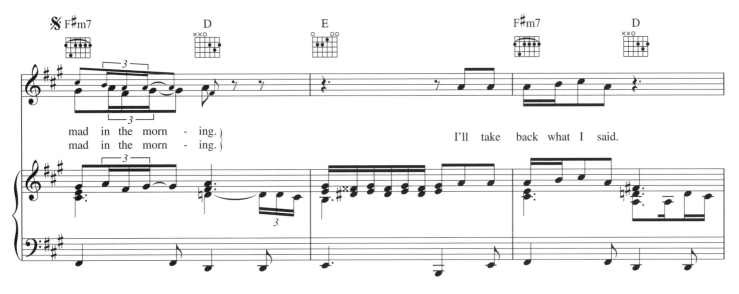

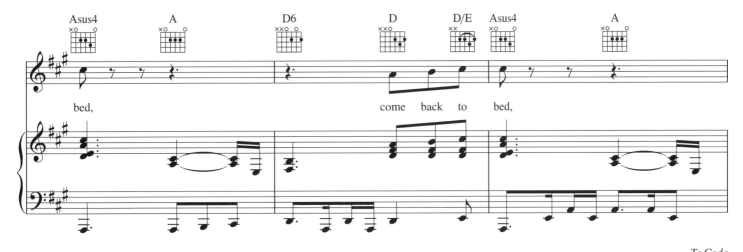

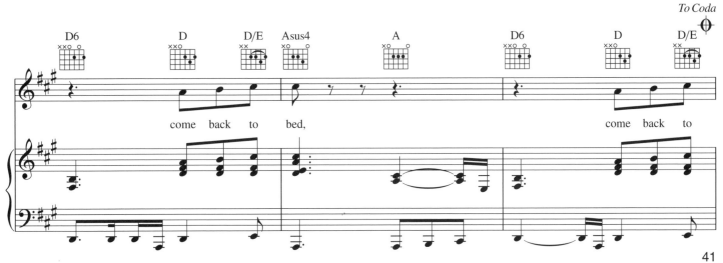

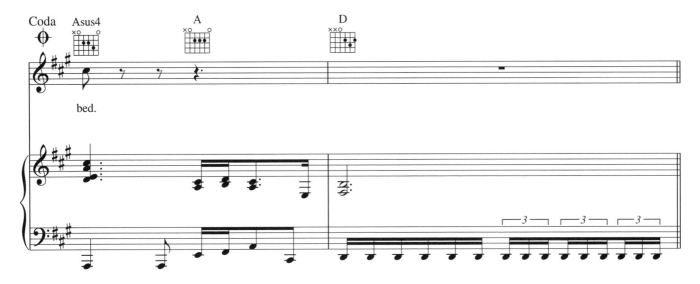

bed.

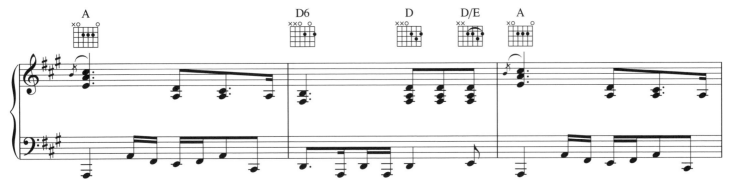

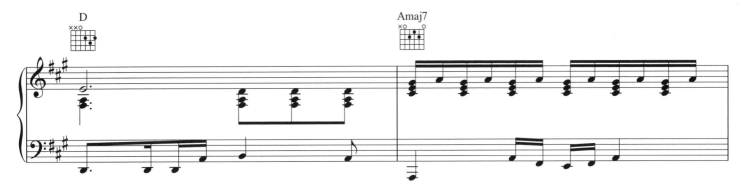

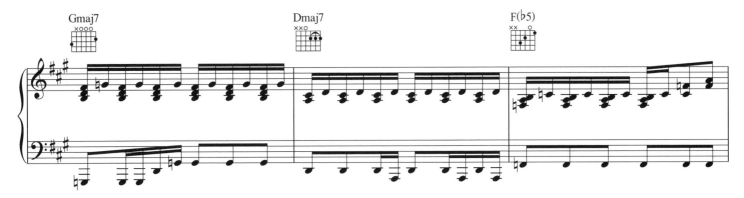

Home Life

Words by John Mayer

Music by
John Mayer and David LaBruyere

Moderately bright

G7sus4

Think I'm gon - na stay home,
want to see the end game.

have my - self a home - life.
want to learn her last name.

Sit - ting in the slow - mo,
Fin - ish on a Fri - day

I

To Coda I

lis - ten - ing to the day - light.
and sit in traf - fic on the high - way.

See, I re - fuse _____ to be - lieve _____
I am not a no - mad.

that my life's
I am not a rock - et man.

just _____ some string of _____ in - com - pletes. _____
I was born a house - cat

by the slight of my moth-er's hand. __ I

𝄋𝄋
G7sus4

think I'm gon-na stay home. I want to live in the

cen-ter of a cir-cle. _____ I want to live on the side of a square. _

I used to be in my "M to Z," now.
I'd love to walk to where we both can talk.

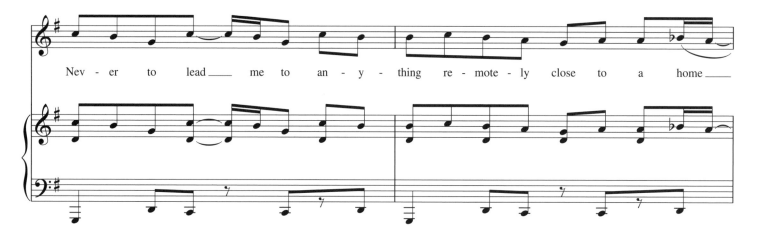

Nev - er to lead ___ me to an - y - thing re - mote - ly close to a home ___

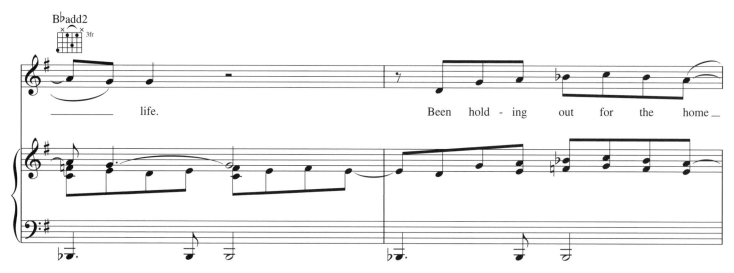

___ life. Been hold - ing out for the home ___

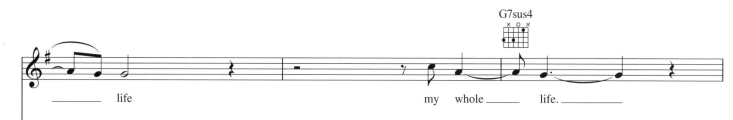

___ life my whole ___ life. ___

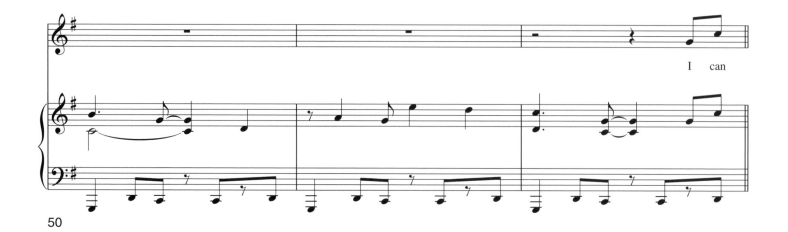

I can

tell you this much. I will mar - ry just once, And if it does - n't work out, give her
go to my grave with the life that I gave, not just some mel - o - dy line on a

half of my stuff. It's fine with me. We said e - ter -
ra - di - o wave. It dis - si - pates

ni - ty. And I will and soon e - vap -

o - rates. But home life does -

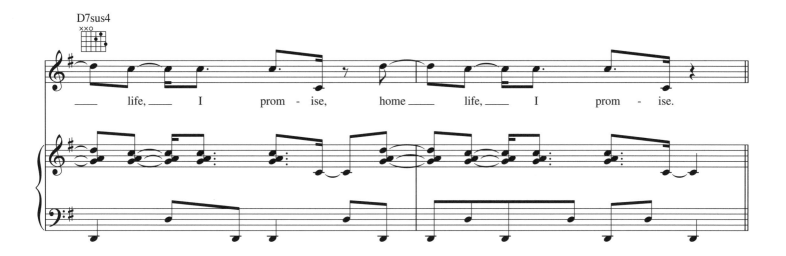

life, _____ I prom - ise, home _____ life, _____ I prom - ise.

Life, _____ home ____ life, _____

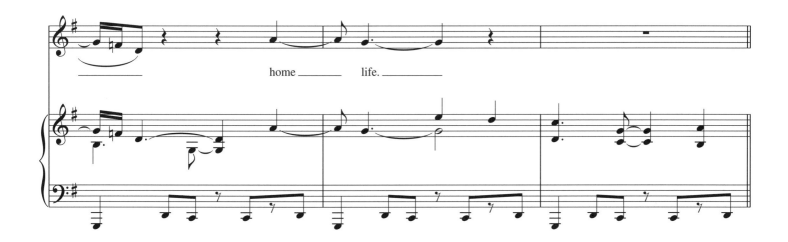

home _____ life. _____

Repeat and fade

53

Split Screen Sadness

Words and Music by
John Mayer

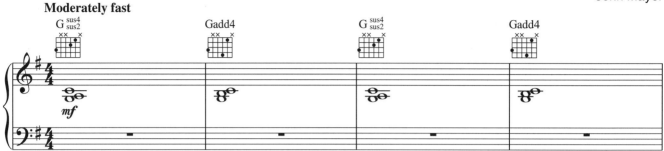

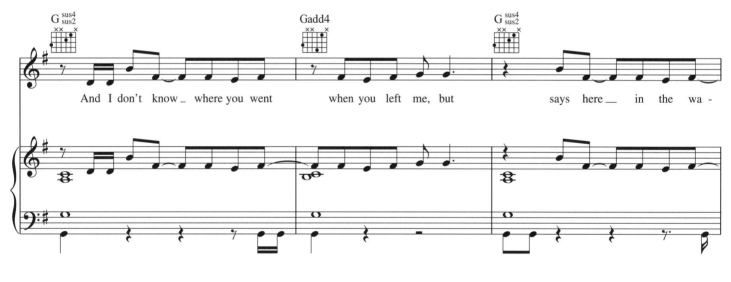

And I don't know _ where you went when you left me, but says here _ in the wa-

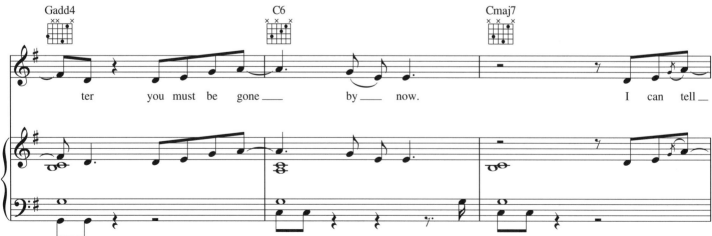

ter you must be gone ___ by ___ now. I can tell ___

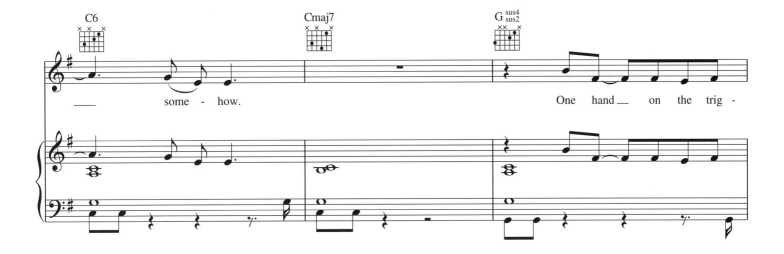

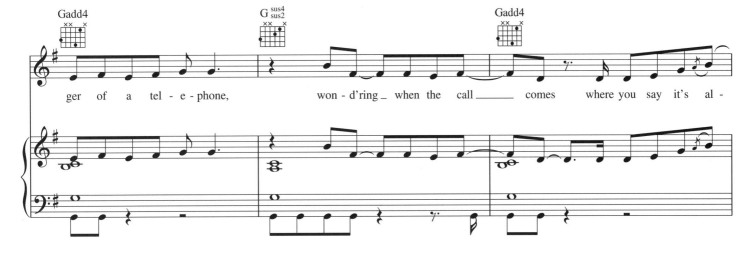

wait on the porch _ till you come _ back home. _ Oh, right. _

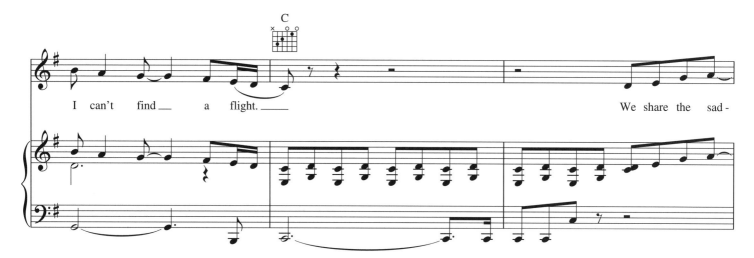

I can't find _ a flight. _ We share the sad-

ness. Split _ screen sad - ness.

Two wrongs make it all al - right _ to - night.

Cmaj9

Two wrongs make it all al - right __ to - night. Two wrongs make it

all al - right __ to - night. Two wrongs make it all al - right __ to - night.

G

"All you need is love" __ is a lie, __ 'cause we had __ love, _ but we still __

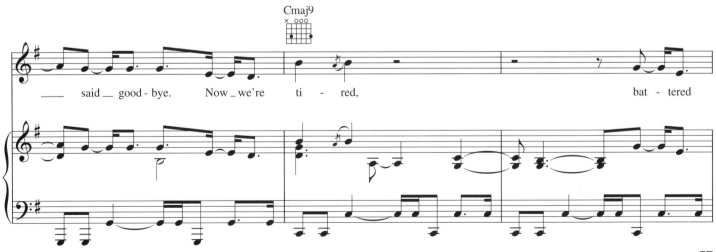

Cmaj9

__ said __ good - bye. Now _ we're ti - red, bat - tered

wait on the porch_ till you come __ back home. __ Oh, right. ___

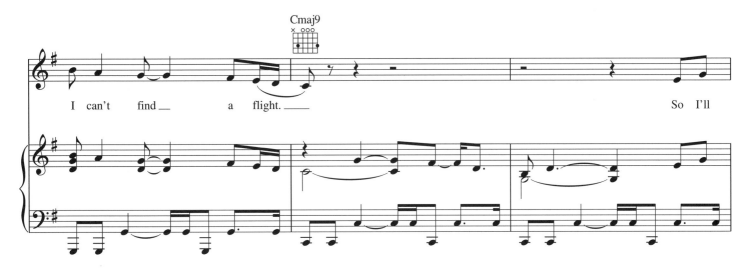

I can't find __ a flight. ___ So I'll

check the weath - er wher - ev - er you are, ___ 'cause I

wan - na know if you can see the stars __ to - night. ___ It might

be my __ on - ly __ right. _____   We share the sad -

ness.

(Two wrongs make it all al - right __ to - night.   Split __ screen sad -

ness.

Two wrongs make it all al - right __ to - night.   We share the sad -

ness.

Two wrongs make it all al - right __ to - night.   Split __ screen sad -

60

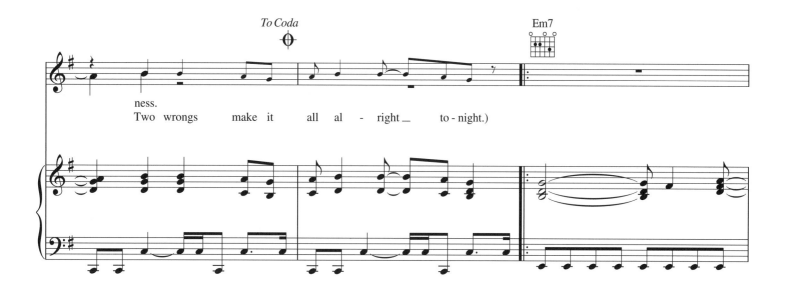

ness.
Two wrongs make it all al - right __ to - night.)

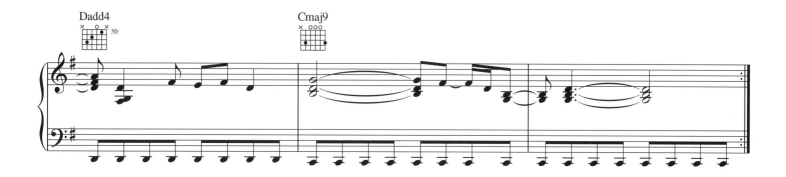

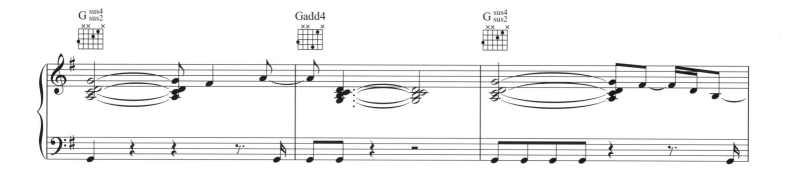

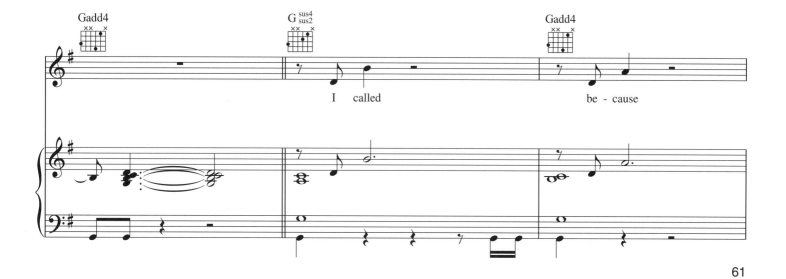

I called   be - cause

61

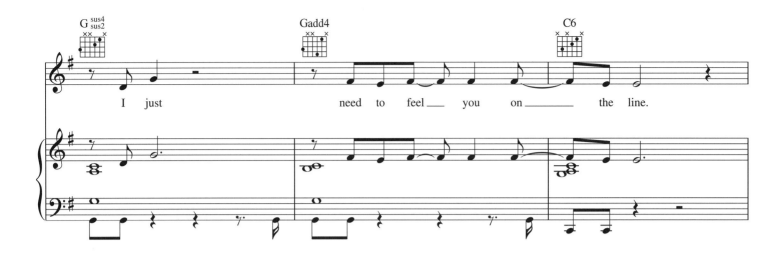

I just need to feel____ you on____ the line.

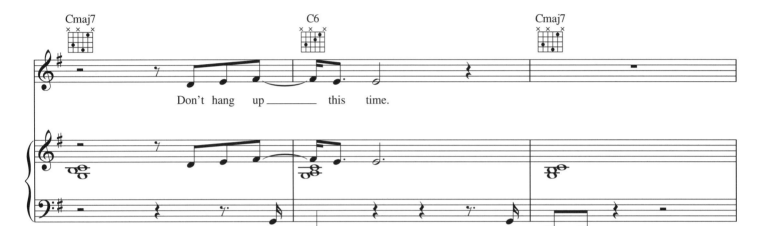

Don't hang up____ this time.

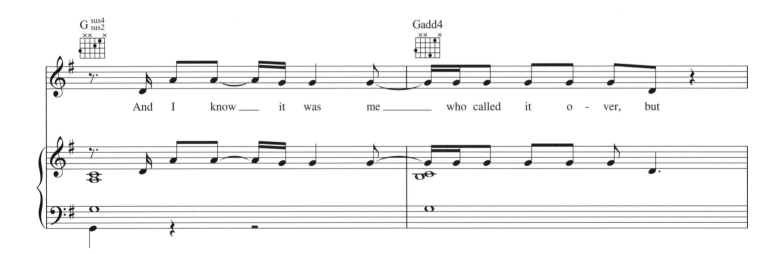

And I know ___ it was me_____ who called it o - ver, but

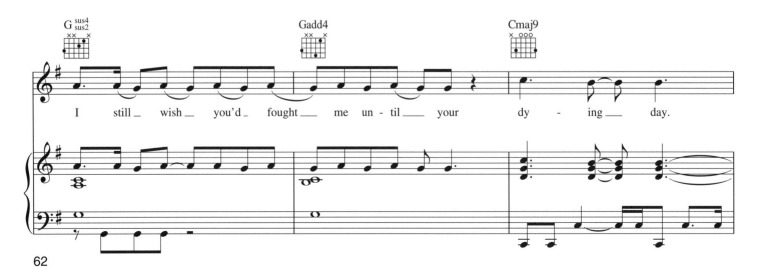

I still_ wish_ you'd_ fought___ me un - til___ your dy - ing___ day.

62

Don't let __ me get a - way. __

Am

'Cause I can't wait to fig - ure out what's _ wrong __ with me

C   G

so I can say this is the way that I used _ to be.   There's no

D.S. al Coda

Cmaj9

sub - sti - tute __ for __ time, __   or for the sad -

Coda

G

Oh, in the sad - ness. It's al - right, ___ it's al -

all al - right ___ to - night.) (Two wrongs make it

right. ___ Oh, in the sad - ness. It's al - right, ___ it's al - right. ___ Oh, in the sad -

all al - right ___ to - night. Two wrongs make it all al - right ___ to - night.

Cmaj9

ness. It's al - right, ___ it's al - right. ___ Oh, in the sad -

Two wrongs make it all al - right ___ to - night.

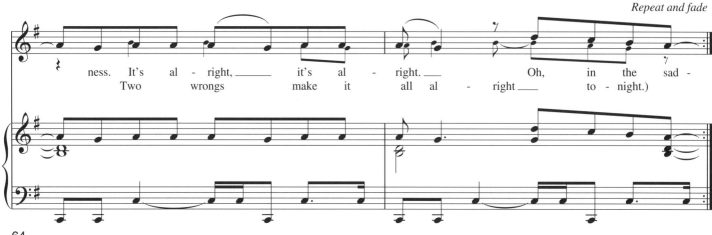

Repeat and fade

ness. It's al - right, ___ it's al - right. ___ Oh, in the sad -

Two wrongs make it all al - right ___ to - night.)

Daughters

Words and Music by
John Mayer

Slowly, in 2

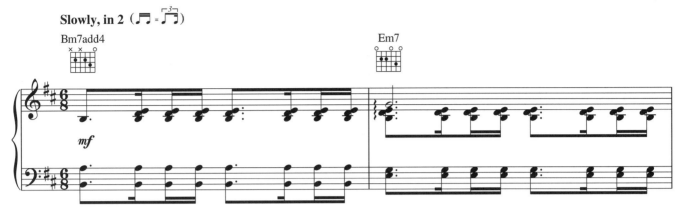

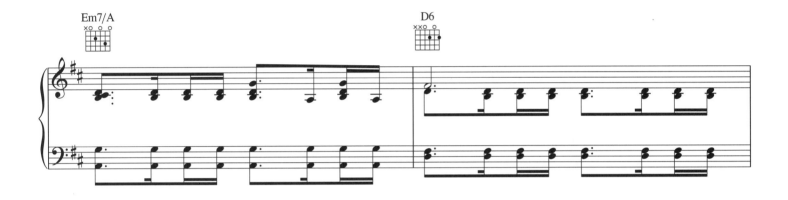

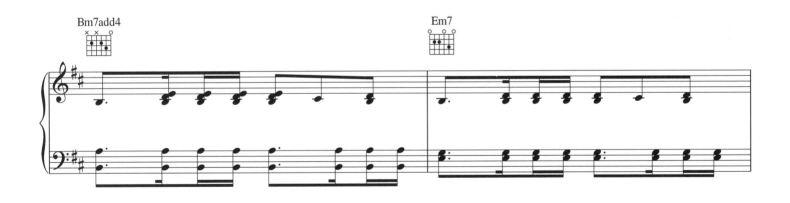

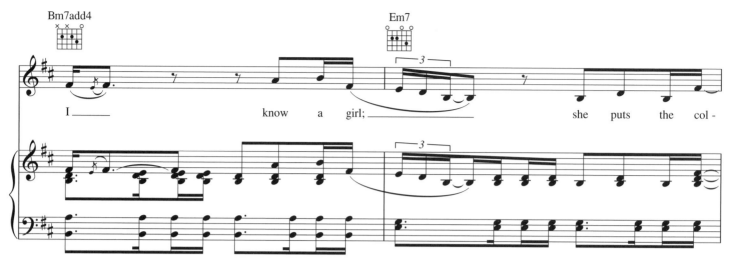

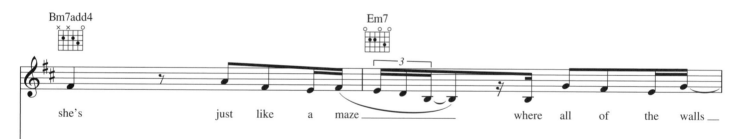

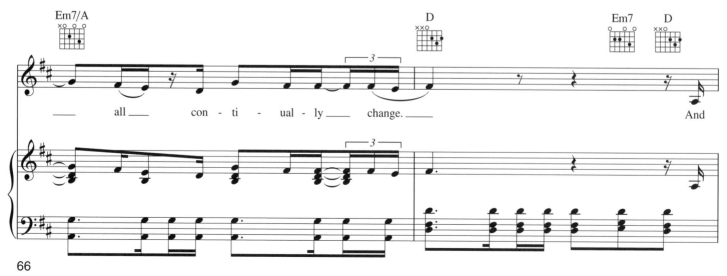

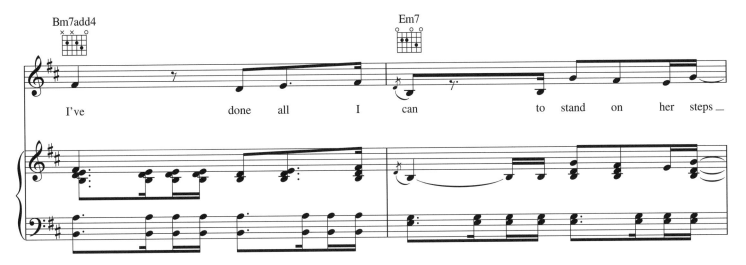

I've done all I can to stand on her steps __

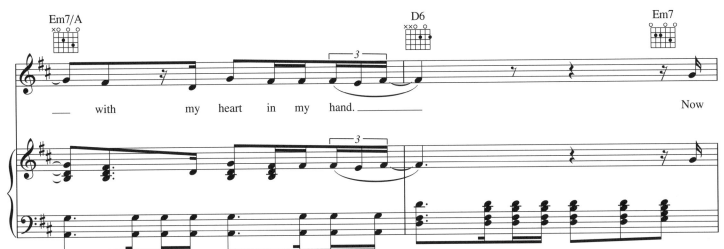

__ with my heart in my hand. _____ Now

I'm start-ing to see may-be it's__ got __

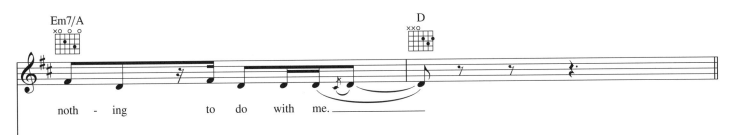

noth-ing to do with me. _____

Fathers, be good to your daughters.

Daughters will love like you do.

Girls become lovers who turn into mothers. So

mothers, be good to your daughters, too.

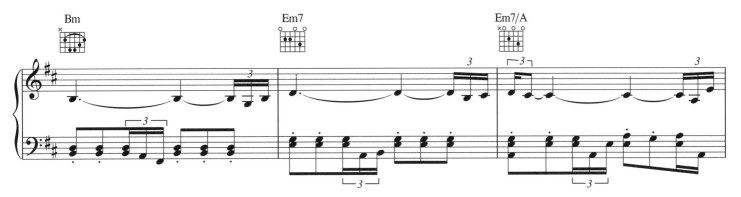

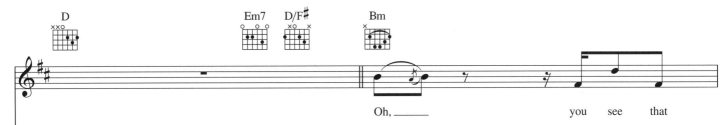

Oh, _____ you see that

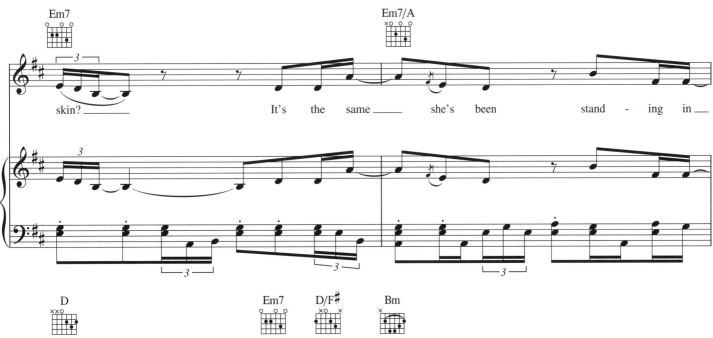

skin? _____ It's the same _____ she's been stand - ing in _____

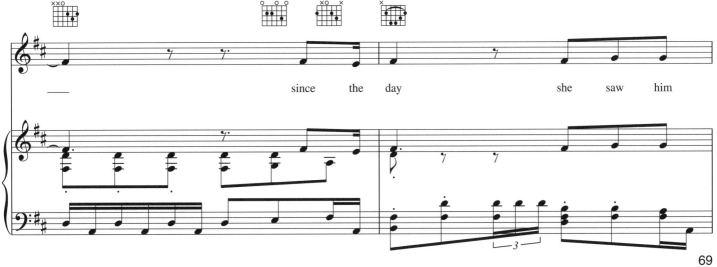

_____ since the day she saw him

but boys would be gone _____ with out _____ warmth _____ from a
wom - an's good, good heart. _____
On be-half of ev-'ry man look-ing out for

71

ev - 'ry girl, you are the god and the weight _ of her

D.S. al Coda II Coda II

world. ___ So daugh - ters, too. So

moth - ers be good ___ to your daugh - ters, too. So

moth - ers be good ___ to your ___ daugh - ters, too. _____

Only Heart

Words and Music by
John Mayer

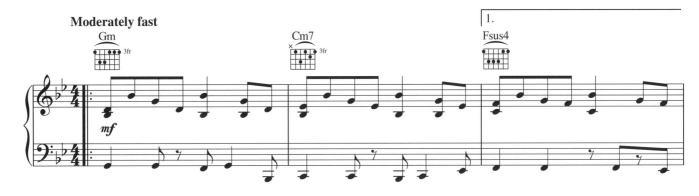

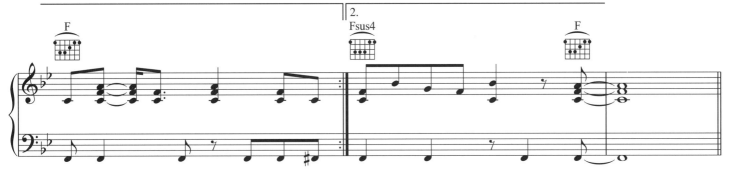

Do not ___ waste this eve - ning. Ba - by, I'm beg - ging you.
It's so hard ___ to be so far out, liv - ing our sep - 'rate lives.

Your big ___ i - mag - i - na - tion's play - ing its tricks ___
Your phone ___ was real - ly bro - ken. I tried your num -

on you

ber twice.

if you think_ my up and

And if you_ need con - fir -

leav - ing's some - thing I'm gon - na do.

ma - tion, ba - by, I un - der - stand.

Feel my chest _ when I look at you. Ba - by, you, _

It's al - right _ if you want me to tell you. You, _

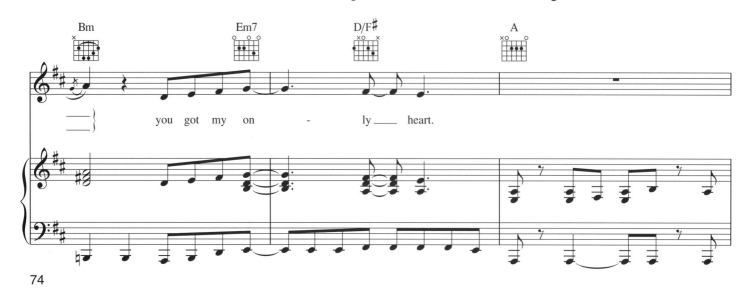

_ you got my on - ly _ heart.

Yeah, _____ you got my on - ly _____ heart.

Yeah, _____ you got my on -

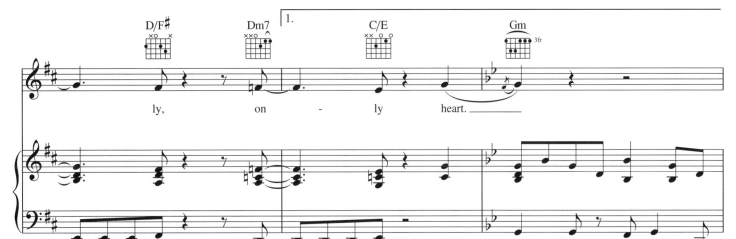

ly, on - ly heart. _____

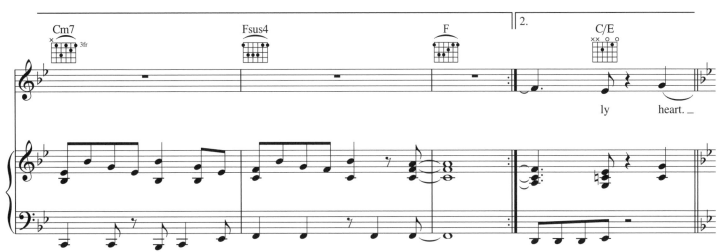

ly heart. __

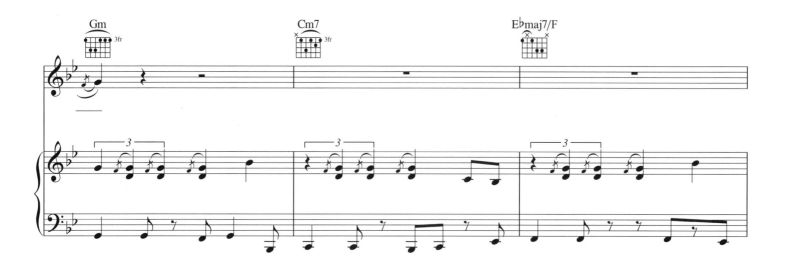

And you love like your hand's on the horn, ba - by.

I a - dore ____ you, but there's a hole

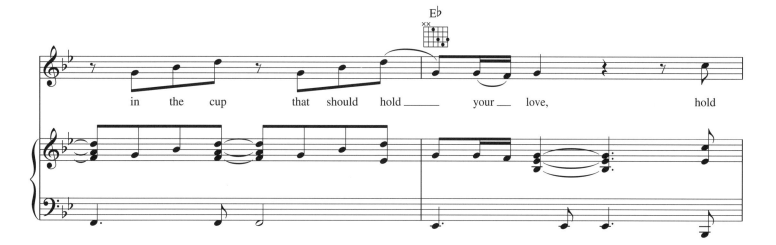

in the cup   that should hold _____ your _ love,   hold

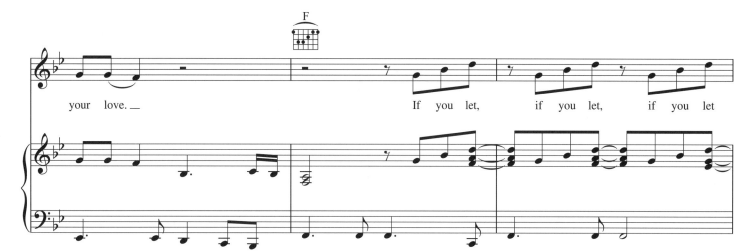

your love. _   If you let,   if you let,   if you let

me leave, _____   I swear   I _____

nev - er _____ will. _____   Oh,   re - mem - ber now,

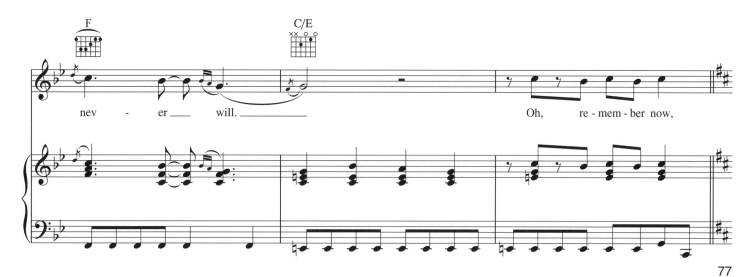

you, you got my on - ly _____ heart.

Yeah, _____ you got my on - ly _____ heart.

Yeah, _____ you got my on -

Repeat and fade

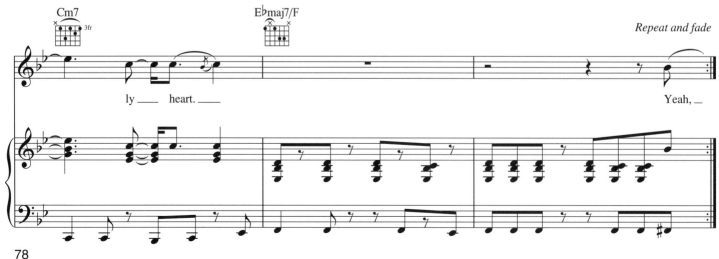

ly _____ heart. _____ Yeah, _

Wheel

Words and Music by
John Mayer

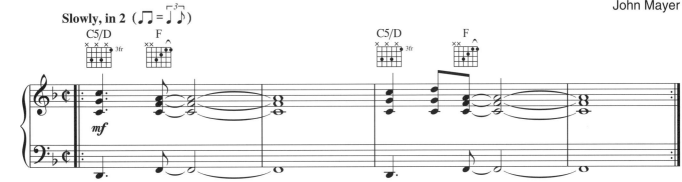

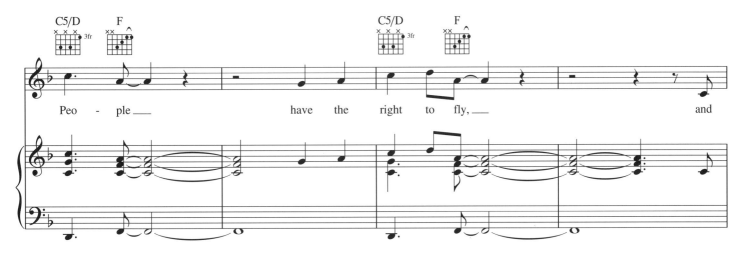

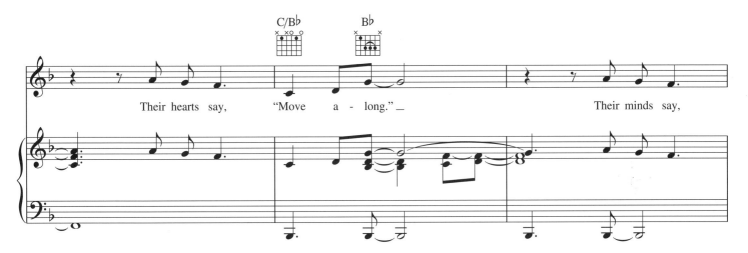

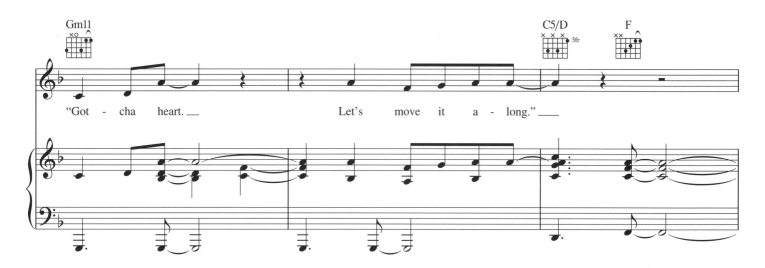

"Got - cha heart. ___ Let's move it a - long." ___

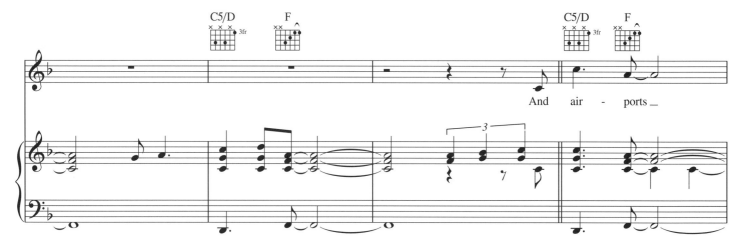

And air - ports ___

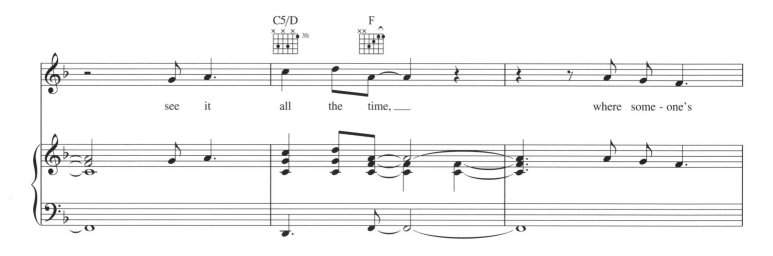

see it all the time, ___ where some - one's

last good - bye ___ blends in with some - one's sigh ___

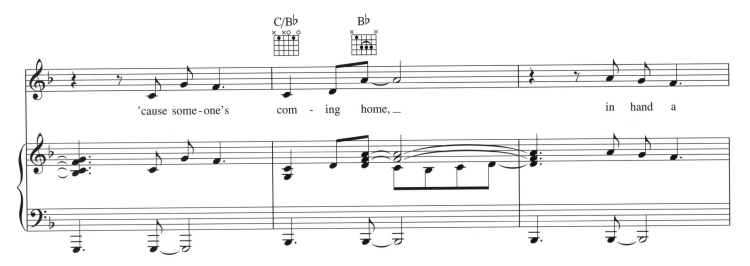

'cause some-one's com - ing home, __ in hand a

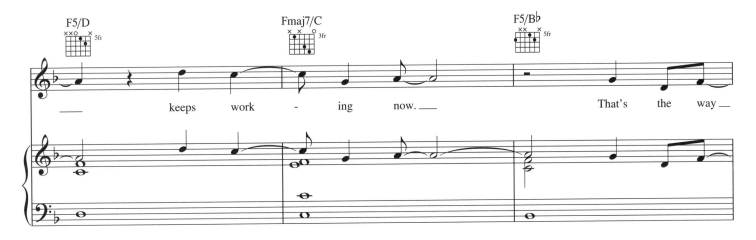

sin - gle rose. __ And that's the way __ this wheel __

__ keeps work - ing now. __ That's the way __

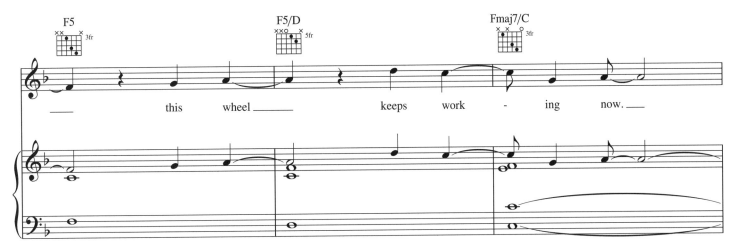

__ this wheel ___ keeps work - ing now. __

And I won't be the last, ___ no, I won't
And you won't be the first, ___ no, you won't

be the last ___ to love her.
be the first ___ to love me.

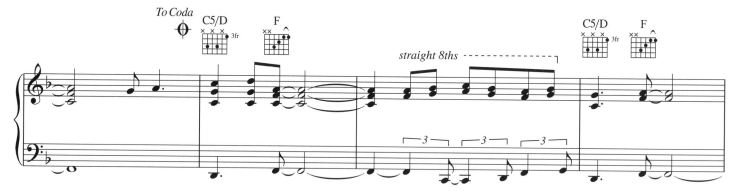

straight 8ths

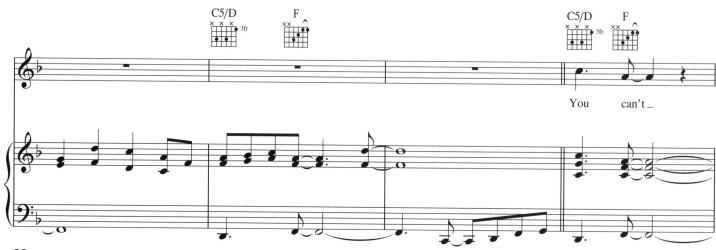

You can't _

build a house of leaves ____ and live like ____

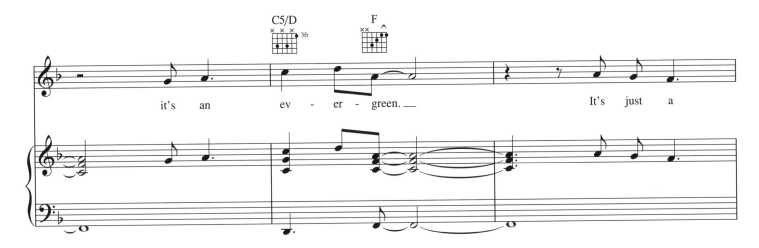

it's an ev - er - green. ____ It's just a

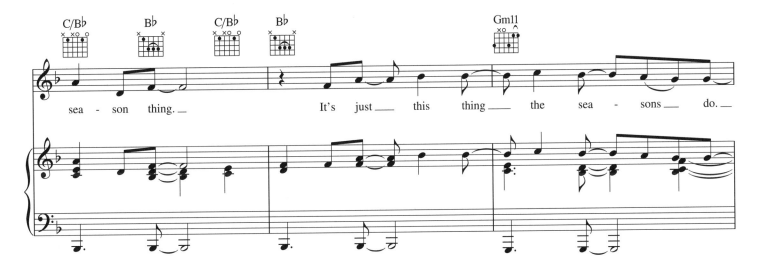

sea - son thing. ____ It's just ____ this thing ____ the sea - sons ____ do. ____

D.S. al Coda

____ And that's the way ____

Coda

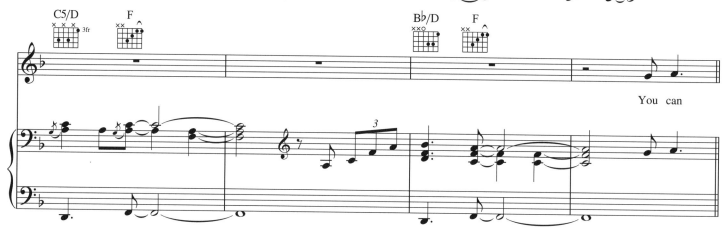

You can

find me ___ if you ev - er want a - gain. ___ I'll be a -

round the bend. ___ I'll be a - round the bend. ___

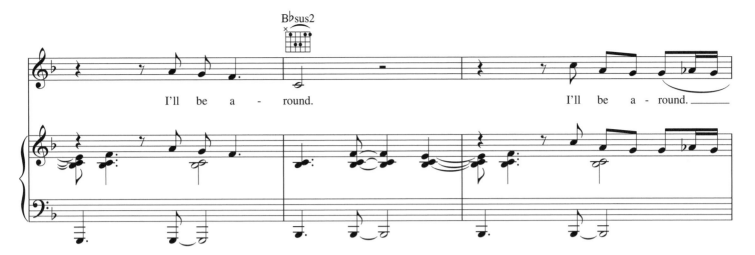

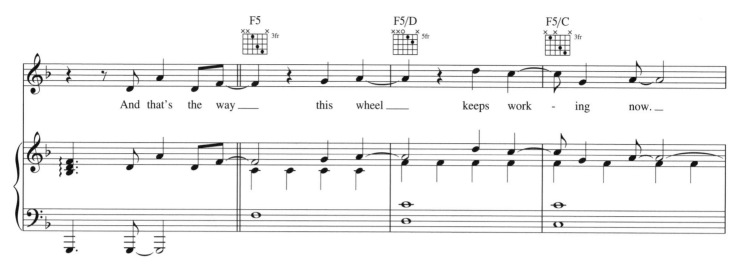

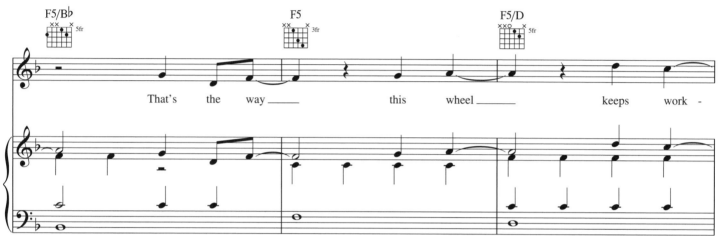

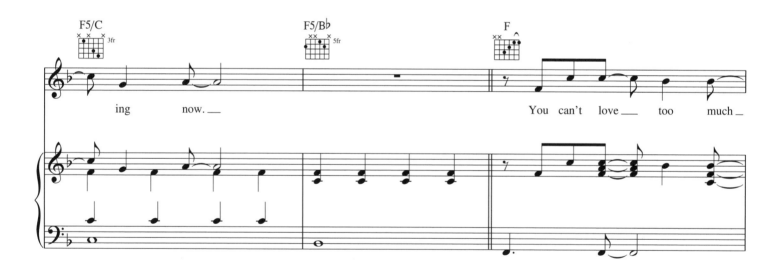

You can't love ____ too much ____ one part ____ of it.

I be - lieve _____ ____ give ____ re - turned ____

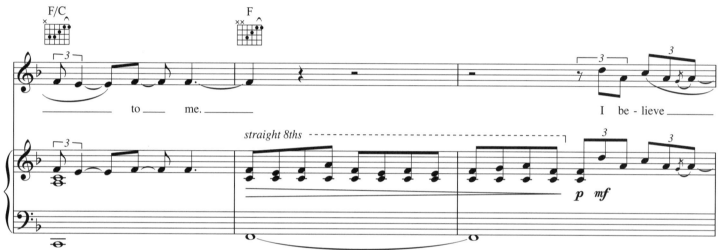

_____ to ____ me. _____

I be - lieve _____

straight 8ths

p *mf*

Freely

Tacet

____ that my life's _____ gon - na see

the love ____ I ____ give ____ re - turned _____ to ____ me. ____